SOCCER

Activity book

ROSA MOSS

This Book Belongs To

_____

_____

The soccer ball is round and ready for action!

It's like a tiny world of adventure, inviting you to kick, dribble, and score goals with your friends.

Remember to share the ball and take turns, showing kindness and respect to everyone on the field.

BALL

Look at the boy bending his knee to give the ball a big kick!

This move is essential in soccer, helping players control the ball and send it flying towards the goal.

KNEE KICK

See the boy running after the ball with all his might?

He's showing great effort and perseverance, never giving up until he reaches his goal.

That's the spirit of never giving up and always giving your best, no matter what.

CHASING
DREAMS

Watch the girl as she reaches out to catch the ball.

She's showing excellent coordination and concentration, just like you when you're focused on a task.

Remember to support your friends, just like she's ready to catch the ball for her team!

GOALKEEPER

Scoring a goal isn't just about points. It's about teamwork, dedication, and fair play.

Celebrate success, but also remember to congratulate others and uphold good sportsmanship values.

GOAL

Don't forget your soccer shoes!

They're like your trusty companions on the field, helping you run, kick, and play safely.

Remember to help others, whether it's tying their shoelaces or offering a helping hand.

SHOES

Imagine winning a trophy for your skills and good sportsmanship!

It's a symbol of your hard work and dedication, reminding you to always strive for excellence.

Remember to congratulate others on their achievements, spreading joy and positivity.

TROPHY

Listen to the referee's whistle, signaling the start or end of the game.

It's a reminder to play with integrity and respect for the rules.

Remember to be fair and honest, both on and off the field.

WHISTLE

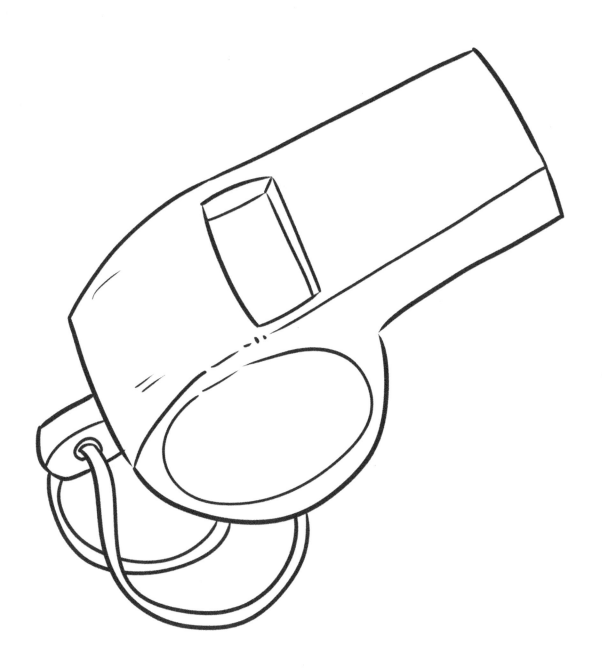

① PLAY FAIR

Always play by the rules and treat everyone with fairness

Cheating isn't playing!

CONNECT THE DOTS

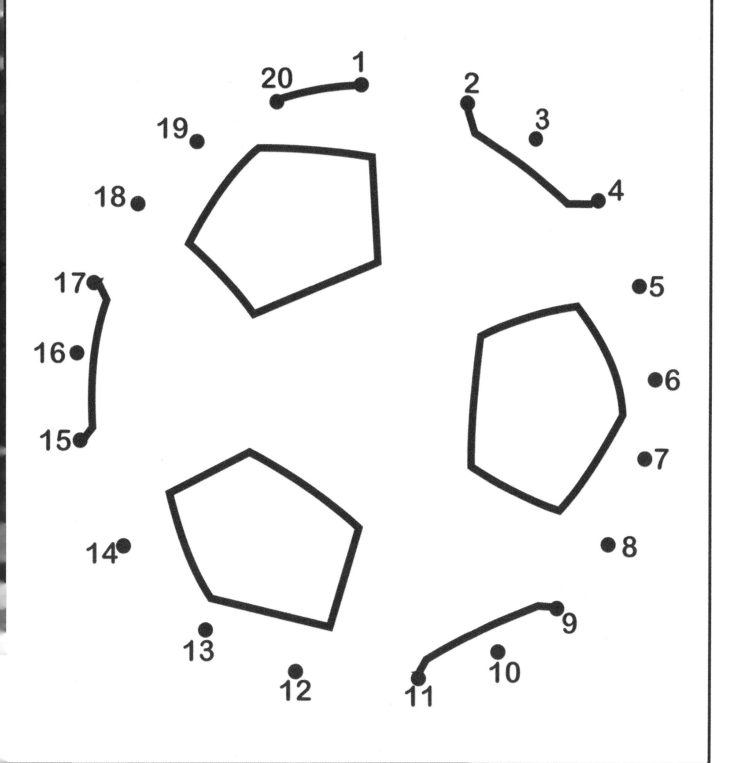

CONNECT THE DOTS

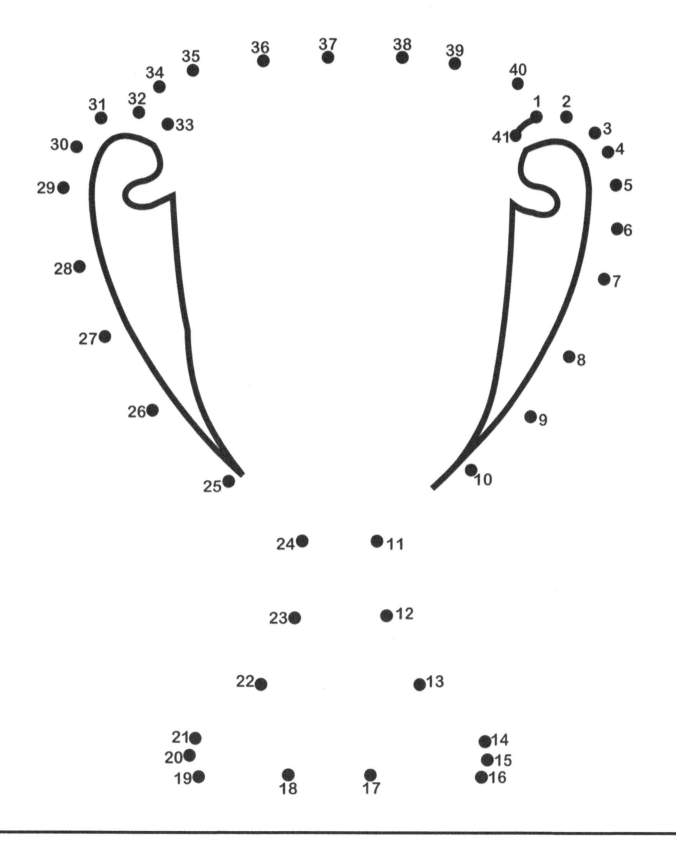

CONNECT THE DOTS

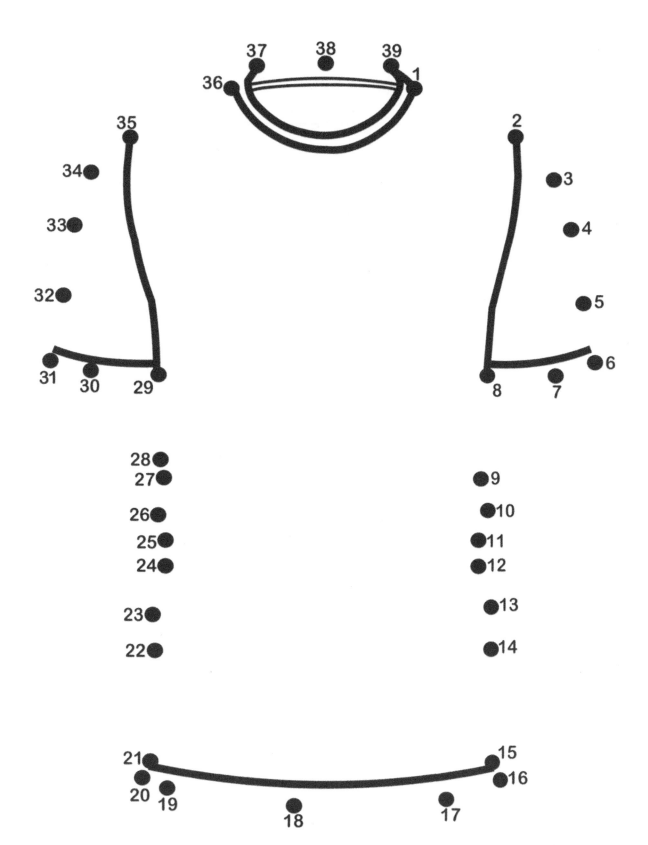

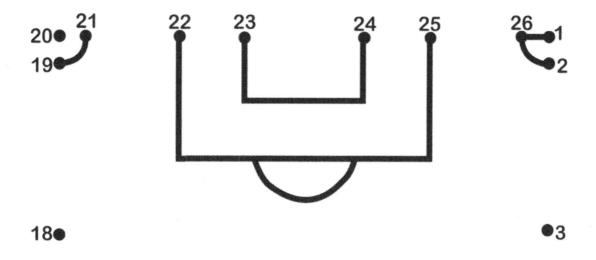

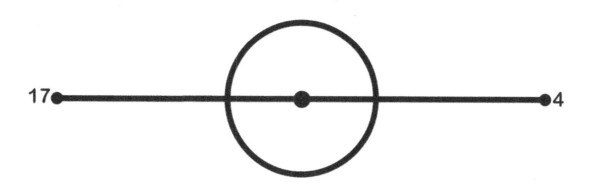

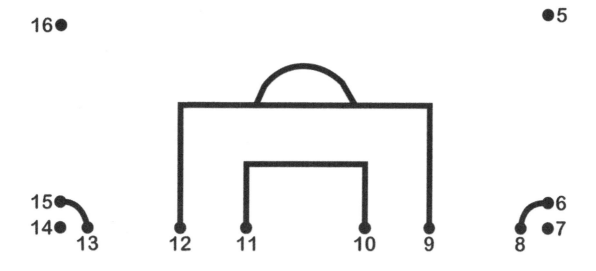

② BE A GOOD ATHLETE

Win or lose, always shake hands and say, "Good game!"

Being a good sport is more important than winning.

SHAPES GAME

Color  Trace  Draw

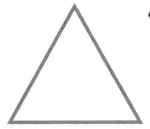

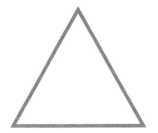

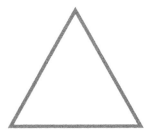
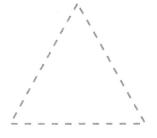

SHAPES GAME

Color  Trace   Draw

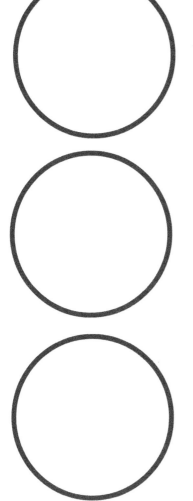

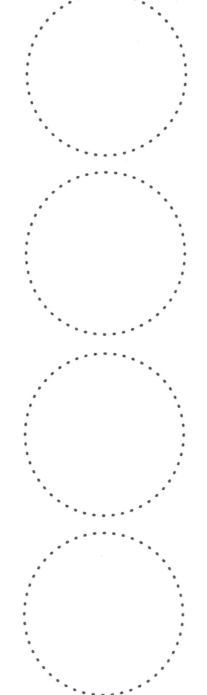

SHAPES GAME

Color 7:0 Trace   Draw

SHAPES GAME

③ CHEER FOR EVERYONE

It's not just about your team

Cheer for all players, whether they're on your team or not

Everyone deserves encouragement!

TRACING LINES

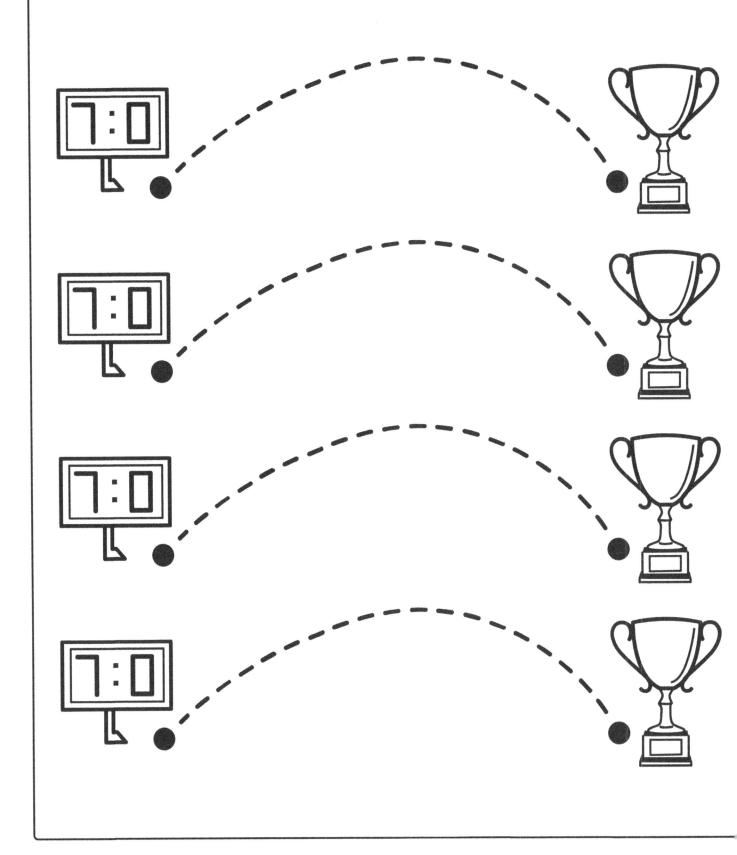

TRACING LINES

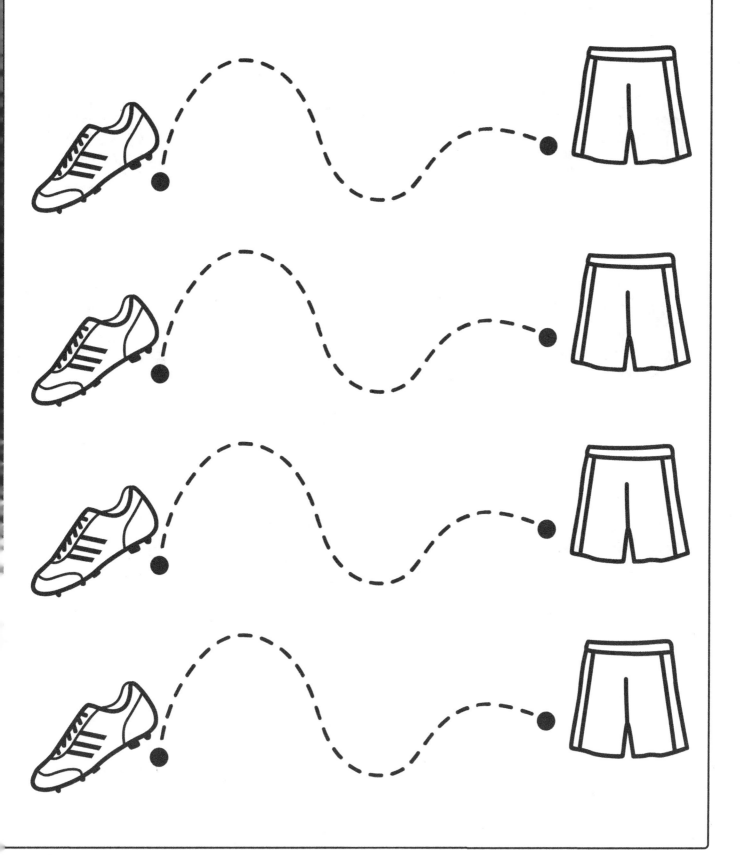

TRACING LINES

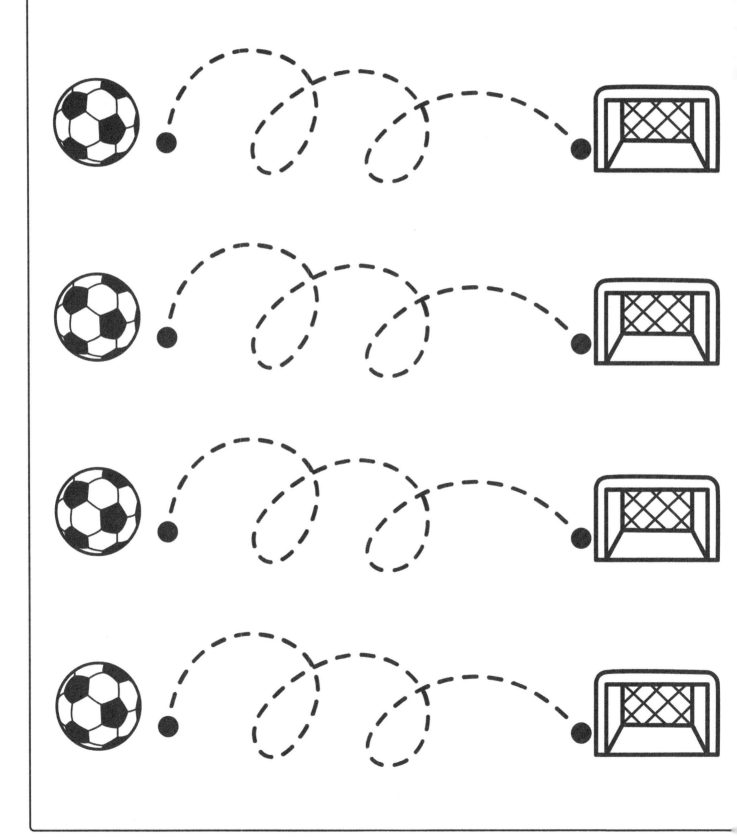

TRACING LINES

(4) LISTEN TO THE REFEREE

When the referee blows the whistle, stop and listen

They're there to keep the game fair and safe for everyone

CIRCLE THE BOX THAT CONTAINS MORE SHAPES

COUNT THE ITEMS AND WRITE THE NUMBER IN THE BOX

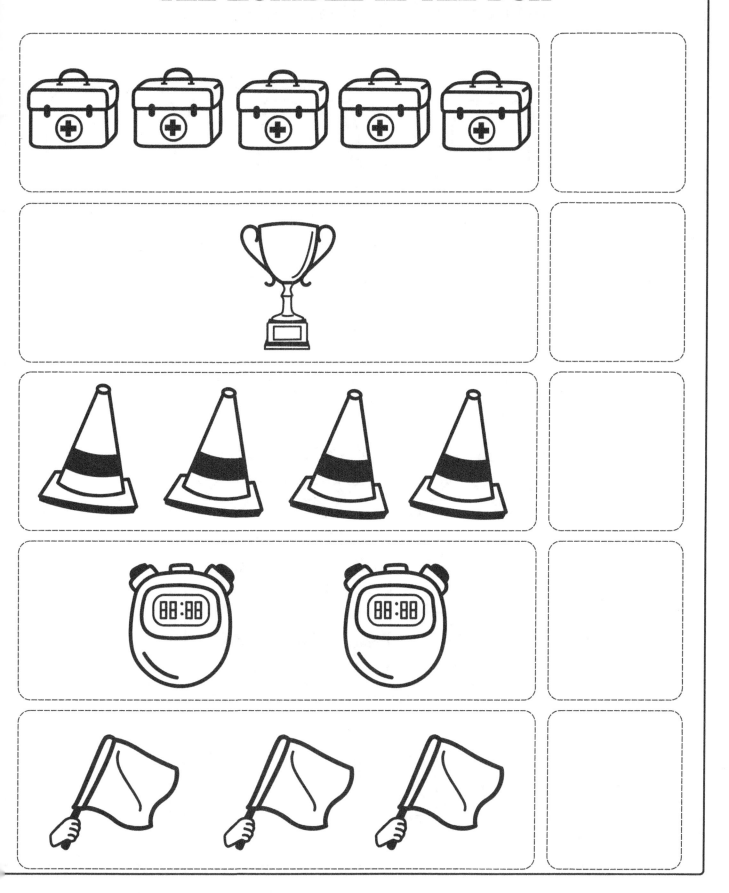

COUNT THE ITEMS AND WRITE THE NUMBER IN THE BOX

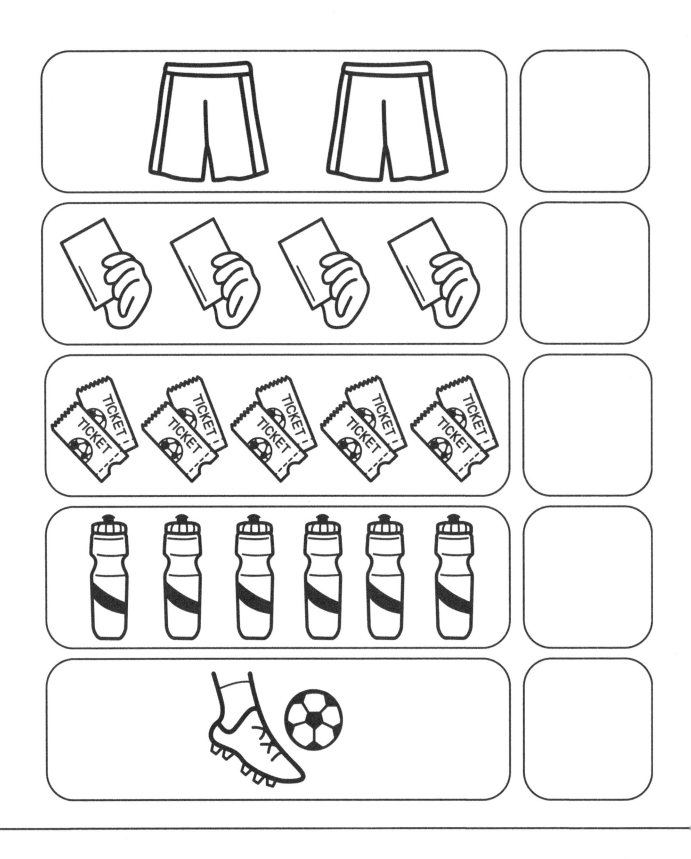

FIND AND COUNT

⑤ HELP YOUR TEAMMATES

Soccer is a team sport

Help your teammates when they need it, and they'll help you too!

COLOR THE SHAPES CORRECTLY

BLUE   GREEN   YELLOW   RED   BROWN

COUNT AND MARK

(4) (1) (3) (2)

(2) (3) (5) (6)

(2) (1) (5) (4)

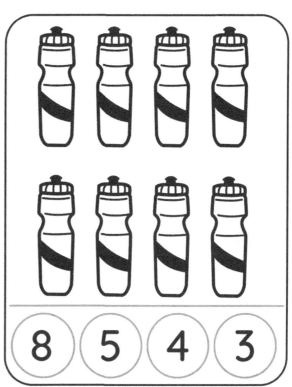

(8) (5) (4) (3)

DRAW A LINE TO CONNECT THE NUMBER TO THE EXACT AMOUNT OF SHAPES

1

2

3

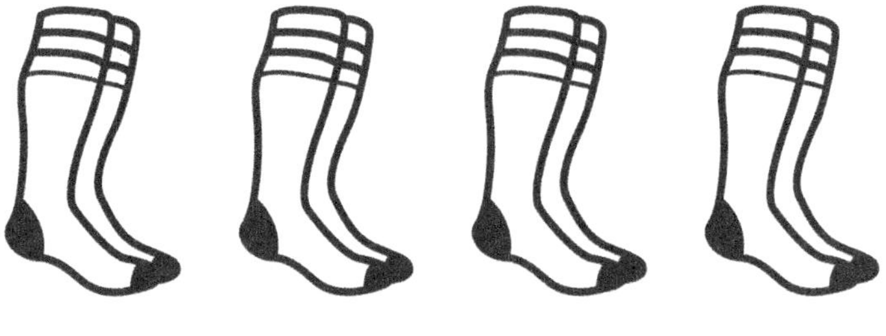

4

5

DRAW LINES TO MATCH THE SAME SHAPES

ROLL THE DICE AND COLOR THE ELEMENT

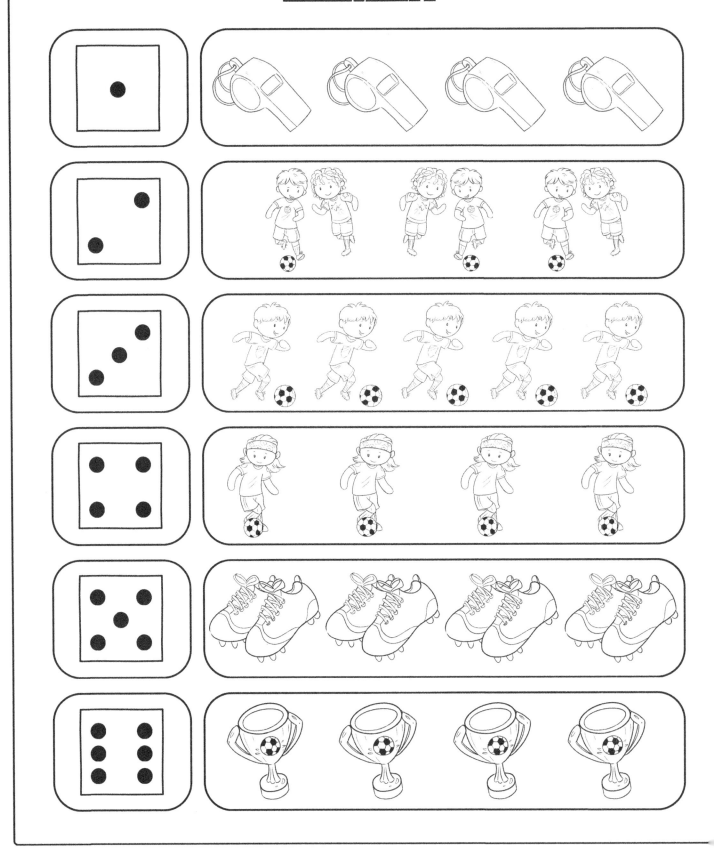

DRAW ONE MORE AND DRAW ONE LESS

(6) RESPECT YOUR OPPONENTS

Treat your opponents with respect

They're playing the game, just like you are

SOCCER MAZE

SOCCER MAZE

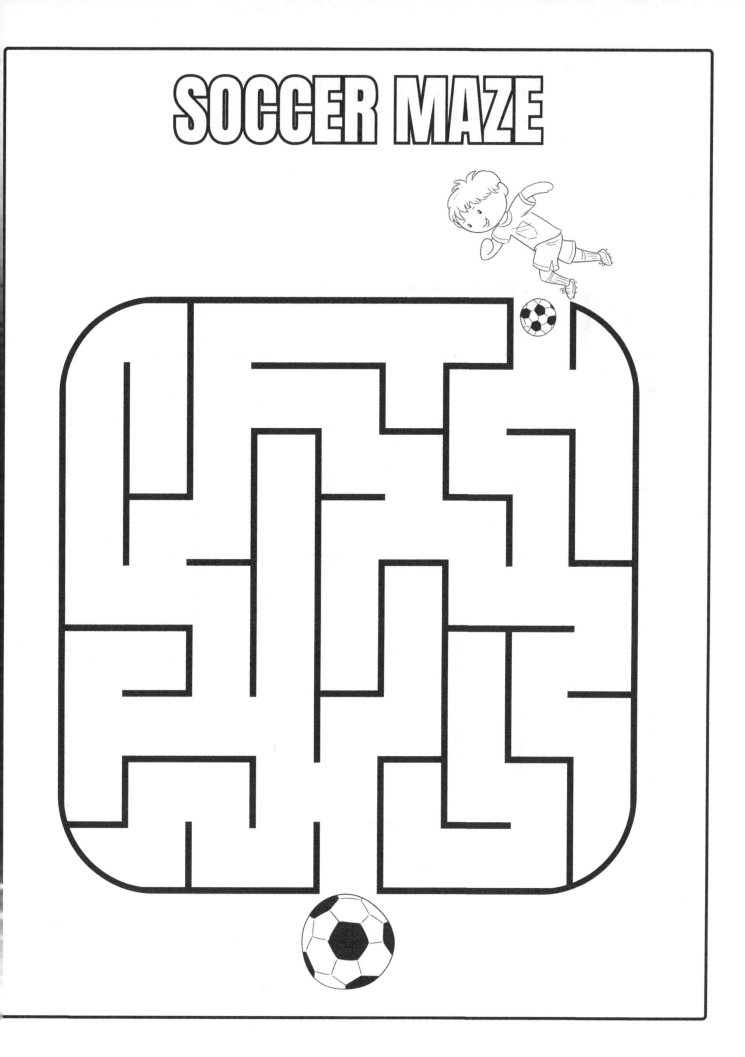

SOCCER MAZE

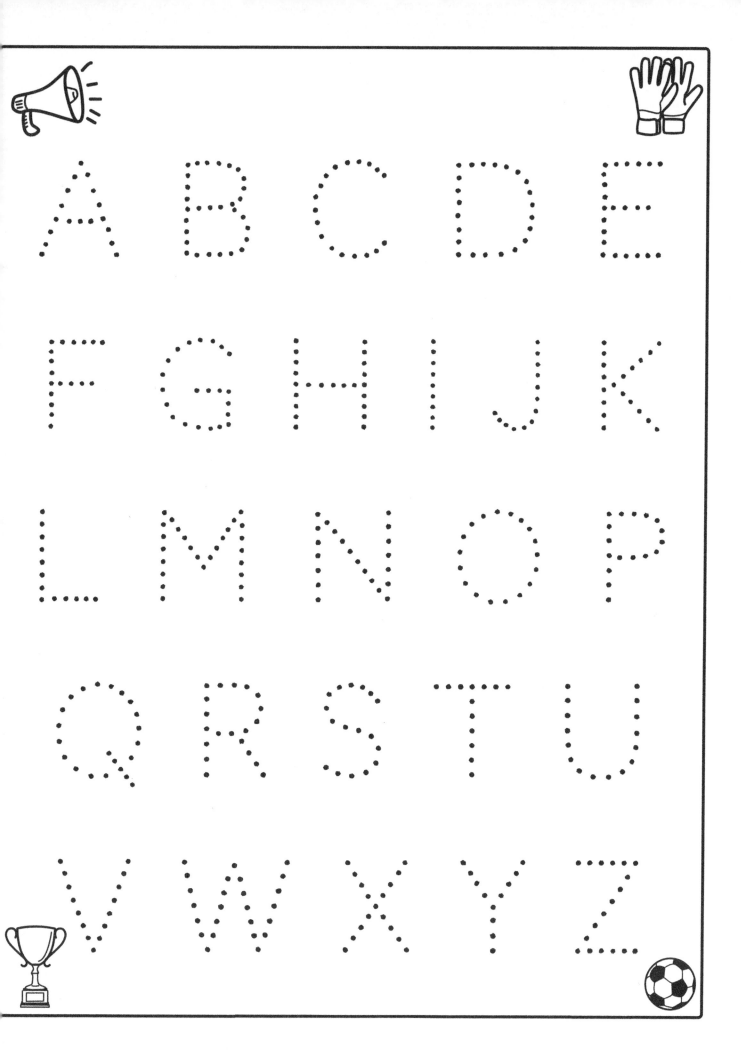

⑦ STAY POSITIVE

Even if things don't go your way, stay positive and keep trying your best

You'll improve with practice and determination

CUT AND SORT
Small to Big

CUT AND SORT
Small to Big

CUT AND SORT
Small to Big

CUT OUT AND PASTE THE NEXT ITEM IN EACH ROW

Certificate

Of Achievement For Kids

★ ★ ★ ★ ★

Name:

Achievement:  Successfully Completing the Soccer Activity Book

_____   _____
Date   **Signature**

Congratulations, Soccer Star!
Keep shining bright on and off the field!

Made in the USA
Las Vegas, NV
26 November 2024

12687208R00044